Walruses

By Valerie J. Weber

Reading Consultant: Susan Nations, M.Ed.,
author/literacy coach/consultant in literacy development

WEEKLY READER®
PUBLISHING

Please visit our web site at www.garethstevens.com.
For a free catalog describing our list of high-quality books,
call 1-800-542-2595 (USA) or 1-800-387-3178 (Canada).
Our fax: 1-877-542-2596

Library of Congress Cataloging-in-Publication Data

Weber, Valerie.
    Walruses / by Valerie J. Weber ; reading consultant, Susan Nations.
        p. cm. — (Animals that live in the ocean)
    Includes bibliographical references and index.
    ISBN-10: 0-8368-9566-5   ISBN-13: 978-0-8368-9566-7 (lib. bdg.)
    ISBN-10: 0-8368-9576-2   ISBN-13: 978-0-8368-9576-6 (softcover)
    1. Walrus—Juvenile literature. I. Title.
QL737.P62W43   2009
599.79'9—dc22   2008013204

This edition first published in 2009 by
Weekly Reader® Books
An Imprint of Gareth Stevens Publishing
1 Reader's Digest Road
Pleasantville, NY 10570-7000 USA

Senior Managing Editor: Lisa M. Herrington
Senior Editor: Barbara Bakowski
Creative Director: Lisa Donovan
Designer: Alexandria Davis
Cover Designer: Amelia Favazza, *Studio Montage*
Photo Researcher: Diane Laska-Swanke

Photo Credits: Cover, pp. 5, 13, 15 © SeaPics.com; pp. 1, 11, 21
© Paul Nicklen/National Geographic/Getty Images; pp. 7, 19 © Norbert Rosing/
National Geographic/Getty Images; p. 9 © Eric Baccega/naturepl.com;
p. 17 © Jeff Lepore/Photo Researchers, Inc.

Printed in the United States of America

1 2 3 4 5 6 7 8 9 10 09 08

Table of Contents

Boldface words appear in the glossary.

Tusks for Teeth

Do you see the big **tusks** on this walrus? Those long white spikes are the animal's teeth! Would you like to brush those teeth every day?

tusks

Walruses use their tusks in many ways. They push the tusks into the ground or ice. Then they pull themselves out of the water.

They use their tusks to fight other walruses. Tusks also help walruses defend against **predators**. Predators are other animals that hunt and eat walruses.

Small Heads, Big Bodies

A walrus's tusks are huge, but its head is small. Behind tiny eyes are small ears. Whiskers hang below the nose. The walrus finds food by feeling with its whiskers.

ear

whiskers

The small head connects to a BIG body. A male walrus can weigh as much as a car! Thick fat called **blubber** keeps the animal warm.

A walrus has two sets of flippers. The animal uses its front flippers to steer. Back flippers push the walrus through the water.

front flippers

back flippers

A Friendly Cuddle

Walruses lie in groups to soak up the warm sun. Sometimes a big walrus climbs over all the other walruses. It wants the best spot on the beach!

Mothers and Babies

Baby walruses are called **calves**. They are usually born on the sea ice. Mother walruses and their calves often stay apart from the **herd**, or big group.

On land, mother walruses hug their babies between their flippers. In the water, calves sometimes travel on their mothers' backs. What a great ride!

Glossary

blubber: a thick layer of fat that keeps sea animals warm

calves: baby walruses or other animals, such as cows, elephants, and whales

herd: a large group of animals

predators: animals that hunt and eat other animals

tusks: long, pointed teeth

For More Information

Books

The Walrus. Creatures of the Sea (series). Kris Hirschmann (Gale Group, 2003)

Walruses. Ocean Life (series). Martha E. H. Rustad (Coughlan Publishing, 2003)

Web Sites

Walruses at Enchanted Learning

www.enchantedlearning.com/subjects/mammals/ pinniped/Walrusprintout.shtml

Check out the diagram of the walrus to learn about the parts of its body.

Ranger Rick: Giants of the North—Walruses

findarticles.com/p/articles/mi_m0EPG/is_n11_v31/ ai_19955858

Learn about walruses' tusks, how the animals dive for their dinner, and their giant sleepovers.

Publisher's note to educators and parents: Our editors have carefully reviewed these web sites to ensure that they are suitable for children. Many web sites change frequently, however, and we cannot guarantee that a site's future contents will continue to meet our high standards of quality and educational value. Be advised that children should be closely supervised whenever they access the Internet.

Index

About the Author

A writer and editor for 25 years, Valerie Weber especially loves working in children's publishing. The variety of topics is endless, from weird animals to making movies. It is her privilege to try to engage children in their world through books.